W9-ANP-936

The Blackbirch Visual Encyclopedia

Natural
Science

BLACKBIRCH®
PRESS

THOMSON
GALE

San Diego • Detroit • New York • San Francisco • Cleveland • New Haven, Conn. • Waterville, Maine • London • Munich

THOMSON

✷

™

GALE

For more information, contact
The Gale Group, Inc.
27500 Drake Rd.
Farmington Hills, MI 48331-3535
Or you can visit our Internet site at http://www.gale.com

Text credit: Claire Aston, Steve Parker

Consultant credit: Steve Parker BSc Scientific Fellow of the Zoological Society

Illustration credit: Susanna Addario, Mike Atkinson, Andrew Beckett, John Butler, Martin Camm, Ferruccio Cucchiarini, Elisabetta Ferrero, Giuliano Fornari, Andrea Ricciardi di Gaudesi, Gary Hincks, Ian Jackson, David More, John Morris, Steve Noon, Nicki Palin, Alessandro Rabatti, Eric Robson, Claudia Saraceni, Peter David Scott, Ivan Stalio, Colin Woolf, David Wright

LIBRARY OF CONGRESS CATALOGING-IN-PUBLICATION DATA

Harris, Nicholas, 1956-
Natural Science / Nicholas Harris.
    p. cm. — (Blackbirch visual encyclopedia)
    Summary: A visual encyclopedia of natural science, including ecology in general and in specific environments, as well as the impact of people on different habitats.
    ISBN 1-56711-523-3 (lib. bdg. : alk. paper)
    1. Ecology—Juvenile literature. [1. Ecology—Encyclopedias.] I. Blackbirch Press. II. Series.

QH541.14.N38 2002
577'.03—dc21   2002018660

Printed in Singapore
10 9 8 7 6 5 4 3 2 1

CONTENTS

ECOLOGY

THE WORD ecology comes from the ancient Greek *oikos (ecos)* meaning "house." It can be thought of as the study of "nature's housekeeping." Ecology looks at how animals, plants, and other living things survive together. It studies how they depend on and relate to each other, such as being plants and plant-eaters, predators and prey, or parasites and hosts. It also examines how living things fit into the environment with their nonliving surroundings including air, water, soil, and rocks, and how they cope with changing conditions such as weather, climate, and seasons.

The green tiger beetle is a fierce hunting insect with large jaws to seize prey such as worms. It is a single organism or individual but it cannot live alone. It needs other animals for food, plants for shelter, and a mate of its kind for breeding.

One of the most important activities living things do is feeding. Plants "feed" on sunlight and minerals from the soil and form the group known as primary producers. Animals that eat plants form another group, herbivores. They range from tiny insects to rabbits. Animals that eat animals are carnivores. When plants and animals are linked in this way, it is called a food chain. Since animals eat more than one kind of food, food chains are part of more complex food webs, such as this example *(left)* from a North American forest.

Ecology is a "new" part of the life sciences. Compared to zoology and botany (the studies of animals and plants), which are thousands of years old, ecology has been carried out in a detailed and serious way for less than one hundred years. It is also a very complex and wide-ranging science, relying on topics such as meteorology (the study of weather and climate) and oceanography. In turn, the basic ideas of ecology are used in related subjects such as farming, pollution control, conservation, and countryside care.

Ecology is divided into various specialist areas such as the freshwater ecology of ponds, rivers, lakes, and marshes; marine ecology of estuaries, seas, and oceans; and terrestrial ecology of the land. Ecologists are interested mainly in what living things—called organisms—do in their surroundings. They think of the natural world as being divided up into ecosystems, distinct areas in which living things interact with their environment. All ecosystems taken together form the biosphere, the living world.

The green tiger beetle is part of the soil community *(below)*. It competes for small prey with others such as centipedes and spiders. It may be hunted itself by larger predators such as shrews or moles. The part or role that an organism plays in its community, in this case as a small predator, is called its ecological niche.

COMMUNITY AND HABITAT

The basic part or unit of ecology is an individual organism, such as an animal or plant. Individual organisms hardly ever live on their own. They exist and interact with others, satisfying their needs such as shelter and nourishment. For example, an animal eats part of a plant, then the plant grows using that animal's droppings as fertilizer.

Living things in an ecosystem that interact and rely on each other for survival form a community. Their natural homes may be small like a garden pond or a rotting log, or extensive, like a lake or forest. These homes are all different types of habitat, places based on similar kinds of plants or physical features such as soil type. Examples are oak woods, salt marshes, coral reefs, sand dunes, or the deep ocean floor. The largest habitats are vast areas known as biomes *(see page 6)*.

Human activities have replaced vast areas of countryside with a mosaic of artificial habitats *(right)*. A hedge is like a strip of woodland, while a river has vegetation along its banks. The rest is fields. Left alone, they would slowly change back to the natural habitat of the region. In the case of the soil community *(above)*, this is broad leaf woodland.

WORLD BIOMES

THERE ARE several large-scale types of biome on Earth, nine of which are featured here. Each is made up of smaller-scale habitats that are generally similar to each other. For example, woodlands of oak, beech, maple, and other broad-leaved trees make up the temperate woodland biome.

POLAR

DESERT

NORTH AMERICA

PACIFIC OCEAN

TROPICAL RAIN FOREST

Each biome is the product of the climate, rocks, and soil of the region. The far north and far south of the earth, covered with snow and ice for most of the year, are polar biomes. Just south of the northern polar lands is the tundra biome. It is too cold for trees, but the upper soil thaws during the brief summer and small plants like mosses and sedges grow. The boreal forest is slightly less cold. Conifer trees can grow in summer and also withstand the heavy snows of winter. Around the world cold, highland regions form the similar mountain biome.

In temperate woodland, the summer is longer and warmer. Broad-leaved trees thrive, although they lose their leaves in winter. Tropical forests grow near the equator where the climate is hot and wet through the year. Where it is drier, savanna grasslands grow, and even less rain produces the desert biome.

Streams, rivers, and lakes make up local freshwater biomes, while swamps and marshes form wetlands. The coastal biome is the narrow strip between land and sea. By far the largest biome is the oceans.

SOUTH AMERICA

ATLANTI OCEAN

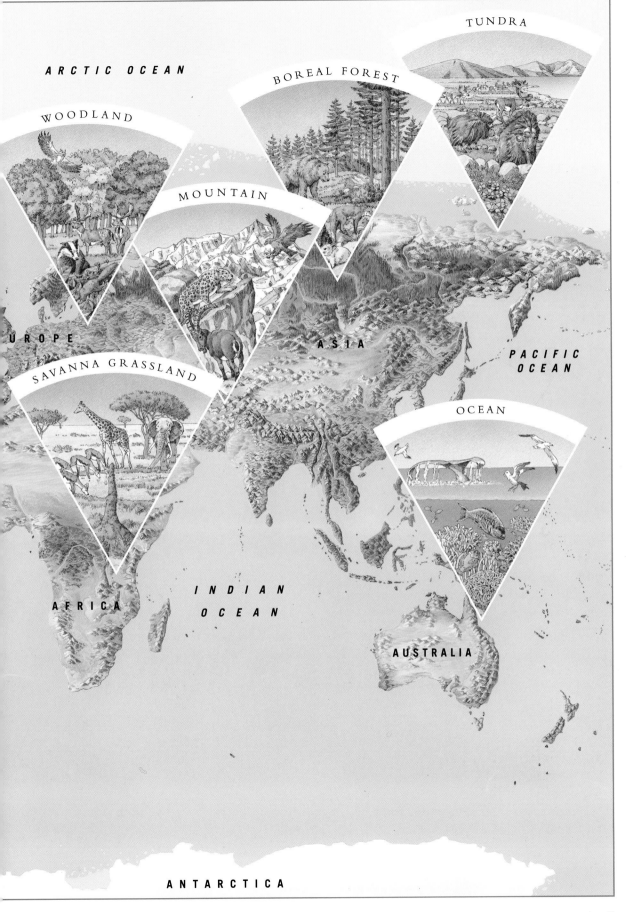

TUNDRA

ARCTIC OCEAN

BOREAL FOREST

WOODLAND

MOUNTAIN

EUROPE

ASIA

PACIFIC
OCEAN

SAVANNA GRASSLAND

OCEAN

AFRICA

INDIAN
OCEAN

AUSTRALIA

ANTARCTICA

NATURAL CYCLES

PLANET EARTH is like a giant, self-contained spaceship. It only has a limited amount of chemical substances and other matter. In nature these chemical elements such as oxygen, carbon, and sulfur are neither made nor destroyed. They are recycled, moving around and around in the natural world in the form of minerals and nutrients. The number of separate pathways and shortcuts is almost endless. But, in general, minerals and nutrients move from the soil into plants, into plant-eating animals or herbivores, then meat-eating animals or carnivores, back into the soil when any plant or animal dies and rots away, and so on. At any time the pathway may branch off, for example, when a scavenger feasts on a rotting animal carcass.

One of the most important chemical substances in nature is carbon. It forms the basis of the building-block molecules of living things, from microscopic cells to our own teeth and hair. In the carbon cycle, carbon in the form of carbon dioxide gas in the air is taken in by plants during the process of photosynthesis and used to build their body parts. Animals eat the plants and rearrange the carbon-based substances to make and maintain their own body parts. At the same time they break down high-energy, carbon-containing substances such as sugars in their bodies, by the process of respiration, to gain energy for their life processes. The respiration combines the carbon from sugar with the oxygen they breathe in to make carbon dioxide gas. This is breathed out into the air—and so the carbon cycle continues.

Plants take up nutrients and minerals through their roots. They use these substances, plus carbon dioxide gas from the air and light energy from the sun, to grow and make new parts.

Herbivore animals eat plants. They take in the plant parts, break them down, or digest them, into minerals and nutrients, and then recycle them to form new parts for their own bodies.

Fungi, microbes such as bacteria, and animals such as worms help the rotting process as plants and animals decay and their minerals and nutrients return to the soil.

Animals produce droppings and eventually they die. Their droppings and bodies become food for scavengers or they begin to decay and rot away.

A slice through the ground reveals the different soil layers *(left).* On top is leaf litter (1) with old leaves, twigs, and feathers. Below is topsoil (2), rich in dead and decaying remains of plants and animals and home to small soil creatures. It also contains the thin roots of small plants. Next is the subsoil (3). This has less organic matter, and more and larger rock fragments. The roots of bushes and trees grow into the subsoil for firm anchorage. The rock fragments get bigger and more numerous until they form solid bedrock (4).

SOIL

SOIL may appear dull and lifeless, but it is a vital part of the natural world. Soil consists of fragments of rock, such as sand grains, mixed with the rotting remains of leaves, animal droppings and other plant and animal matter. Water and air occupy the spaces between the soil particles. Also inhabiting the soil are millions of microscopic living things, such as bacteria, tiny animals like mites and springtails, the roots of growing seeds and full-grown plants, the threads of fungi, small creatures such as earthworms and insect grubs, and larger animals like moles. Soils vary enormously in their thickness, particle size, and the main minerals and nutrients they contain. The climate, the kinds of rocks that lie beneath, and the main types of plants that grow in soil all affect its character and its nourishing ability, or fertility.

Tiny red mites (1), springtails (2), and false scorpions (3) teem in their millions in soil among the plant roots.

Deep soil with plenty of rotting plant and animal matter is very fertile and many plants grow in it. But specialist plants like cacti can grow even in thin, dry, nutrient-poor, sandy desert soils. Sadly, acid rain caused by pollution has made large areas of soil too acidic to support much life.

9

TROPICAL RAIN FOREST

AREAS OF tropical rain forest are found near the equator, in regions with a hot climate and high level of rainfall all year round. The most extensive rain forests are found in central Africa, South America, Southeast Asia and the island of Madagascar. There are also small areas of rain forest in Australia and Central America.

Tropical rain forests are the richest of all environments in terms of plant and animal life. Today, large areas of rain forest are being cut down, both to supply the timber industry and to make room for farming, roads, quarries, and housing.

Lemurs are found in the rain forest of eastern Madagascar. They leap from tree to tree on their long legs, or search for food on the ground.

fruits, and flowers. Below the emergent layer is the canopy, an almost continuous "roof" of branches and foliage. Here, in the warm sunlight, fruits and flowers grow, and many animals feed on them.

Lower still is a shadier area known as the understory, where animals fly, leap, climb, or glide between the trees. Smaller plants that could not survive on the dark forest floor root themselves in pockets of decaying matter among branches, using the trees as a support to reach up toward the light.

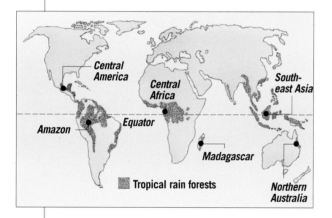

The rain forest is made up of several different layers, like the stories of a skyscraper. At the highest level is the emergent layer, made up of the tallest trees, some of which can reach 230 feet (70 m) in height. This is a bright, windy layer, where birds and bats swoop, feeding on insects,

The mandrill, a kind of baboon, lives on the floor of the central African rain forest.

There are millions of insects in tropical rain forests. Many kinds are as yet unidentified. Some, such as the Queen Alexandra's birdwing butterfly *(left)*, grow to enormous sizes.

At the level of the forest floor, little light can penetrate down through the thick canopy. The atmosphere is dark and still, and ground vegetation is scarce. Only in places where a tree has fallen to create a clearing, or along the banks of a river, can ground vegetation find enough light to grow.

The Amazon rain forest is the largest in the world. It is home to the jaguar, which hunts large mammals such as peccaries and tapirs, as well as to the 30-foot (9-m)-long, river-dwelling anaconda.

KEY
1 *Harpy eagle*
2 *Howler monkey*
3 *Toucan*
4 *Morpho butterfly*
5 *Anaconda*
6 *Tapir*
7 *Scarlet macaw*
8 *Jaguar*

Foliage constantly falls down onto the forest floor from the trees above, forming a layer of decaying plant matter. This is quickly broken up by insects that live and feed among it, so that it becomes a rich source of nutrients for the surrounding trees to take into their roots. The insects themselves are food for birds and ground-dwelling forest animals, such as rodents and lizards. These small animals are, in turn, hunted by larger predators, such as snakes and cats, some of which will often lie in wait on low branches, ready to drop down on to their unsuspecting prey.

Much of the wildlife of the Amazon rain forest is found close to the river.

Large plant-eaters such as elephants and gorillas also feed on the forest floor, pulling foliage from the lower branches. Rivers full of fish run through the forests, and are sources of food and water for many animals. Some animals, like the capybara, also leap into the water to escape from predators.

RAIN FOREST CANOPY

THE CANOPY is where most birds, insects, monkeys, and other rain forest animals live. Many plants, called epiphytes, grow in the moss collected in tree branches. This illustration is of the Southeast Asian rain forest.

Insect-eating birds such as swifts and bee-eaters perch on the topmost branches, ready to swoop down and catch their prey in mid-air. The heavier hornbill sits on lower branches, feeding on fruits.

KEY
1 *Crested swift*
2 *Whiskered tree swift*
3 *Red-bearded bee-eater*
4 *Great hornbill*
5 *Colugo*
6 *Siamang gibbon*
7 *Fruit bat*
8 *Great Memnon butterfly*
9 *Blue-rumped parrot*

The continuous network of branches in the canopy means that some animals hardly ever descend to the ground. There is plenty of food in the form of fruits and leaves, as well as insects and other small life. To move from branch to branch, colugos spread flaps of skin along their body and glide. Gibbons have very long arms and legs, grasping hands and feet. They swing through the trees with a smooth, hand-over-hand movement known as brachiation.

The year-round supply of fruit and flowers provides a feast for fruit bats. While feeding on flower nectar, they also play a part in the process of pollination, as their fur becomes dusted with pollen which is then carried to another flower.

The rain forest canopy is alive with color, provided not only by the fruits and flowers, but also by many brightly colored animals. Huge butterflies flap through the trees, so large that they could almost be mistaken for birds. Groups of noisy parrots provide vivid splashes of color as they search for nuts to crack with their strong beaks.

AMAZON RIVER LIFE

THE AMAZON RIVER has thousands of tributaries that flow through the rain forest. Some of these channels are wide and deep, while others are narrow, shallow, and full of fallen leaves, branches, and winding tree roots. The river teems with fish, including predators such as the notorious piranha, the electric eel, and the arawana, which will often leap out of the water to snatch insects or even birds.

KEY
1 *Piranhas*
2 *Electric eel*
3 *Jacana*
4 *Striped leporinus*
5 *Arawana*
6 *Hummingbirds*
7 *Postman butterfly*
8 *Bromeliad*
9 *Angelfish*
10 *Hyacinth macaw*
11 *Owl butterfly*
12 *Amazon kingfisher*
13 *Tetras*
14 *Bird-eating spider*
15 *Leafcutter ants*
16 *Sunbittern*
17 *Pirarucu*

The river is the hunting ground of birds such as the jacana and the sunbittern. The jacana can walk across floating water plants without sinking, while the sunbittern wades through the muddy shallows, probing for insects and small fish with its long beak. The Amazon kingfisher sits on an overhanging branch. In a flash, it dives into the water, emerging with a fish which it takes back to the branch to eat.

The river channels also provide a rich source of food and water for land-dwelling animals and the peoples of the Amazon. During the rainy season, vast areas of the forest floor flood, and fish swim among the tree trunks. Some animals, such as the capybara, anaconda, or jaguar, are good swimmers and are easily able to negotiate the floodplains. Other animals, such as monkeys, iguanas, and anteaters, take to the trees during the floods.

Fiddler crabs scavenge in the mud at the water's edge. Their huge claws are used to attract a mate or threaten a rival. In the shallows, the archer fish spits a jet of water at insects or spiders that are sitting on leaves above the surface, making them fall into the water.

MANGROVES

MANGROVE FORESTS are found on sheltered, tropical coastlines. They are formed in places such as the mouths of rivers, where flowing salt water lays down mud and other deposits, resulting in swampy land. The roots of mangrove trees are flooded with salt water when the tide comes in. To avoid drowning, mangrove trees have shallow root systems, that branch up above the water line. This allows them to breathe and also acts as a support for the rest of the tree. The tangled mass of roots traps nutrient-rich mud which provides food for many kinds of animals.

The trees and plants of a mangrove forest are home to numerous insects, while many kinds of fish swim through the shallow water between the tangled roots. Crabs, snails, and other small creatures burrow into or crawl across the mud. These animals provide food for frogs and a wide variety of birds. Several kinds of monkey clamber between the trees, feeding on fruits and leaves. They are constantly on the lookout for large predators, such as snakes and crocodiles, which slip through the water or bask on the mudflats.

In the mud left between tides, a fish called the mudskipper skips along on its fins. It breathes using water stored in a chamber near its gills, and can also take in oxygen through its skin. At high tide, most mudskippers retreat into their burrows under the mud. Those left above ground often climb trees to avoid predatory fish.

On the coastline of Southeast Asia, the rain forest merges into mangrove swampland. Wading birds such as storks feed on crabs and fish, while smaller birds hunt for insects and snails. The proboscis monkey (so-called because of the male's long, drooping nose, or proboscis) clambers through the trees. It will swim through flooded areas of forest, but must beware of hungry tigers, crocodiles, and giant snakes.

KEY
1 Rafflesia
2 Tiger
3 Reticulated python
4 Proboscis monkey
5 Banded pitta
6 Gavial
7 Milky woodstork
8 Mudskippers

SAVANNA

SAVANNA grasslands are found close to the equator, outside the belt of tropical rain forests. The largest and best-known savanna grasslands are in Africa, although there are also areas in South America, India, and

KEY			
1 Elephant	6 Zebra	9 Warthog
2 Cheetah	7 Marabou	10 Lion
3 Wildebeest	stork	
4 Giraffe	8 Hyena	
5 Thomson's		
gazelle		

northern Australia. Savanna is dominated by grass, but the landscape is also scattered with bushes and trees. The climate is hot, with a dry season followed by a rainy season.

The vast expanses of grass in the African savanna support a wide range of grazing animals such as wildebeest, zebras, and gazelles. Other plant-eaters, such as elephants, giraffes, and black rhinoceroses, are browsers, feeding on vegetation from bushes and trees. Both browsers and grazers avoid competition for food by feeding at different levels. The giraffe's long neck and the elephant's trunk allow them to reach up to the highest leaves, while smaller animals feed lower down. Among the grazers, zebras and buffalos tear off the coarse top shoots of the grass. The wildebeest then feed on the leafy layer below, leaving the tender shoots at the base for the gazelles.

Most of the African plant-eaters live in herds, for protection against predators. They move from place to place, according to where grass and water can be found. When the dry season begins, they migrate in a vast mass from their breeding grounds in the south to wetter areas in the north and west.

HUNTERS AND SCAVENGERS

The herds of plant-eaters provide food for many savanna carnivores, including lions, leopards, cheetahs, hyenas, and wild dogs. The larger carnivores can kill large plant-eaters such as wildebeest. Smaller, less powerful hunters feed on antelopes and gazelles, rodents, and other small animals. Birds of prey swoop down on their victims out of the sky, or from treetops.

After the hunters have eaten their fill, the scavengers move in. As well as making their own kills, hyenas scavenge from the remains of others, their strong jaws able to crush even bones. Vultures spot the carcass as they circle in the skies, and come down to feed, drawing the attention of other scavengers, marabou storks and jackals. The final scraps are removed by flies and beetles.

Insects are very important to life on the savanna, especially in this "clearing up" process. Dung beetles remove animal dung, on which they feed and lay their eggs. Termites take dead plant matter into their nests, where they grow fungus on it to eat.

Among the top predators of the African savanna are lions. A group, or pride, of lions is mostly made up of females and their young. At the head of the pride is one male, or several related males. The females do most of the hunting, while the males defend the pride's territory. Rival males often battle with each other fiercely for control of a pride.

DESERTS

WITH LITTLE or no rainfall, and often searingly hot temperatures, deserts are some of the most inhospitable places on earth. Some deserts, especially those close to the equator, are hot all year round, with temperatures sometimes reaching 122°F (50°C). Others, such as the Gobi desert in Mongolia, are cold and windswept. There, high mountains act as a barrier to any warm, moist air currents, and temperatures can fall to -4°F (-20°C) in winter.

Many deserts are bare and rocky with areas of sparse scrubland, where only the hardiest plants can grow. As plants need water to survive, they must conserve as much as they can. Desert plants such as cacti have adapted the way they carry out photosynthesis, opening their stomata (pores) to take in carbon dioxide only in

North American deserts are scattered with cacti, some kinds of which can grow up to 49 feet (15 m) in height. Small mammals emerge from their burrows at night to feed, and are themselves hunted by large lizards and snakes. Wild horses roam the deserts, visiting waterholes to drink.

KEY
1 *Wild horses*
2 *Kit fox*
3 *Roadrunner*
4 *Sidewinder*
5 *Gila woodpecker*
6 *Saguaro cactus*
7 *Gila monster*
8 *Kangaroo rat*
9 *Scorpion*

the cool of the night. Their thick, swollen stems also help to reduce water loss. Other desert plants keep most of their bulk in root systems underground, out of the sun's heat.

Some hot deserts are sandy, and the wind sweeps the sand into huge wavelike dunes. In these arid, bare landscapes, the sand is mostly too unstable to support plant life. Sometimes an underground water source comes close to the surface, creating an oasis, where plants can grow, and people can live.

"Living stones" are southern African desert plants. They have very thick leaves with a waxy surface to prevent as little water as possible being lost from them. This means that they can store large amounts of water in their leaves. They live among rocks, taking in any water that seeps into the rock crevices. To avoid being eaten by thirsty animals, these plants have evolved shapes and colors which, when they are not in flower, make them look very much like the surrounding rocks.

The addax is a large antelope from the Sahara desert. Its light-colored coat reflects heat, while its digestive system can cope with coarse grasses and little or no water.

Despite the barren landscape, a surprising variety of animal life can be found in the desert. The biggest problems facing these animals are the heat and the lack of water. Small mammals such as kangaroo rats and ground squirrels spend the day sheltered from the hot sun underground, coming out to feed only at night. Reptiles, on the other hand, need to warm up in the sun before they can become active enough to hunt, so they cannot feed at night. Instead, they find shelter in burrows or rock crevices during the hottest part of the day, basking and feeding during the cooler early morning and evening.

Some large mammals, such as camels, have thick coats on their backs to keep out the heat, and thinner hair on their bellies which lets excess heat out of the body. They can also conserve water inside their bodies, needing to take in very little to survive. Some carnivorous animals get all the water they need from their food, while birds can fly long distances in search of water.

Flowering heathland borders the scrubland desert or "outback" of Australia, where honey opossums sip flower nectar with their brushlike tongues.

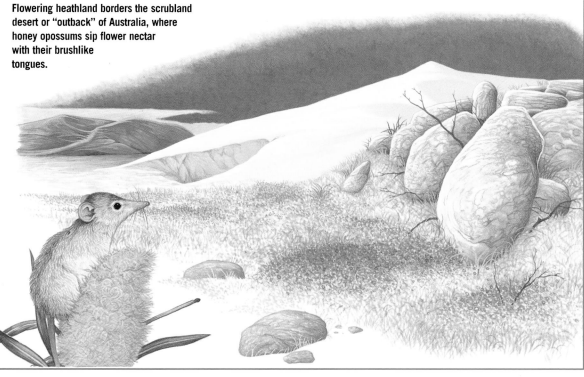

GRASSLANDS

AREAS OF grassland are found in the continental interior, far from the cool, moist winds of coastal areas. This gives them a warm, dry climate in summer, but many also endure cold winters. Because of the lack of rain in the summer, hardy grasses are the main plant life, though trees can also be found where water gathers during spring. The steppes of Asia and the prairies and pampas of North and South America are dominated by grasses, while the African savanna and Australian grasslands, with their tropical climates, have more trees.

Eucalyptus trees *(right)* are found in the Australian grasslands. In the hot, dry conditions, many trees are destroyed by fire, but eucalyptus trees are able to regrow quickly from dormant buds "stored" in their bark.

Grassland animals from four continents *(below)*. The pronghorn of North America, ostrich from Africa, and kangaroo from Australia rely on speed to escape from predators, but the armadillo of South America has protective armor plating.

Pronghorn

Armadillo

Gray kangaroo

Ostrich

Baobab trees of Africa *(below)* survive the dry season by storing water inside their huge, bottle-shaped trunks. They can measure 164 feet (50 m) around their girth.

Grasslands all over the world make ideal environments for plant-eating animals of all sizes, from huge bison to small rodents. The large grazing animals are preyed upon by wolves, coyotes, foxes, and other members of the dog family. Even swift kangaroos sometimes fall victim to packs of wild dogs called dingoes. Smaller plant-eaters, such as rabbits or prairie dogs, are a quick meal for larger hunters, but are also hunted by weasels, badgers, and birds of prey.

In the warm summer months, new varieties of flowering plants and grasses grow on the grasslands, attracting many insects. These provide extra food for small mammals such as ground squirrels, as well as for animals that are primarily insect-eaters, such as armadillos.

During the past hundred years or so, large areas of grassland have been destroyed by humans. This is most evident in North America, where the prairies have been greatly damaged and reduced in size by crop and cattle farming. Animals such as the North American bison and its European relative were hunted almost to extinction.

BELOW GROUND

On the open grassland, where there are few places to hide, the larger grassland animals protect themselves against predators by living in herds. Others rely on speed to carry them away from danger. For the smaller animals, however, the best defence is to live underground. Rabbits, ground squirrels, and cavies burrow networks of holes and tunnels, which they use to sleep in, to escape from predators, and to keep their young safe. As they dig, they also help to mix the nutrients in the soil, and keep the grassland healthy.

Prairie dogs, a kind of ground squirrel, live on the North American prairies, in colonies sometimes numbering hundreds of animals. While feeding on the surface, they will bark at the sight of a predator such as a coyote or bird of prey. Old burrows are often used by other animals such as burrowing owls and rattlesnakes.

WOODLANDS

WOODLANDS are found in parts of the world that have a temperate climate, with warm summers but cool winters. In western Europe, the eastern United States and eastern Asia, woodland is mainly deciduous. In winter, the trees lose their leaves and shut down their growth. This allows them to

Autumn in European deciduous woodland *(below)*. Hedgehogs and dormice feed before hibernating, while squirrels and jays store nuts for the winter. Owls and foxes look out for prey.

KEY
1 *Red squirrel*
2 *Green woodpecker*
3 *Tawny owl*
4 *Dormouse*
5 *Roe deer*
6 *Grey squirrel*
7 *Jay*
8 *Badger*
9 *Rabbit*
10 *Stoat*
11 *Blackbird*
12 *Great tit*
13 *Song thrush*
14 *Fox*
15 *Hedgehog*

conserve water and survive the cold. Further north are the coniferous, or boreal, forests of Russia and North America. Their trees have needlelike leaves and a conical shape to shed heavy snow that could break their branches.

The plants and animals that live in the woodlands also have to survive the winter. Food becomes scarce as plants die back and fruits and seeds are no longer abundant. Some animals hibernate in sheltered tree holes or underground burrows, only stirring with the new growth of spring. Others store enough food during the autumn to last them through the winter.

Unlike the dense roof of a tropical rain forest, the canopy of a deciduous wood lets some light reach the woodland floor, creating a layer of thick, varied ground vegetation. In damp areas, rich green moss coats the trees.

During autumn, fallen leaves build up into a thick layer on the ground, providing insects, worms, and small mammals with a warm hibernation site. There is always danger, however, from digging predators such as foxes. In the spring, insects and other invertebrates feed on the leaf litter, breaking it down into nutrients in the soil, where it is taken up by growing plants.

CONIFEROUS WOODLANDS

Conifers constantly lose and replace their leaves, or needles, throughout the year. The dead leaves are not broken down into the soil because worms and other soil-enriching invertebrates find them distastful. Instead, they remain as a thick layer of leaf litter, making the soil acidic and poor.

Forest berries and fungi provide food for birds and mammals. Crossbills use their specially adapted beaks to open pine cones and reach the nutritious seeds inside. Conifer trees provide animals with shelter and some warmth during the winter.

At one time woodlands covered huge areas of Europe, North America, and Asia. Much deciduous woodland has been cut down to grow crops on its rich soil. Areas of coniferous forest, with its poor soil, still remain in Asia and North America.

The vast coniferous forests of northern Russia are known as the taiga. During the winter, animals that feed on the northern tundra during the short summer, such as elk and reindeer, shelter in the forest, scraping away the snow to feed on mosses. The lynx and goshawk prey on small mammals. The brown bear hibernates until spring.

KEY
1 *Goshawk*
2 *Elk*
3 *Brown bear*
4 *Reindeer*
5 *Lynx*
6 *Crossbill*

A woodland may seem to be a calm, quiet place, but studied closely, it is a hive of activity. A deciduous woodland during the spring and summer months *(right)* is particularly busy. The newly emerged leaves on the trees are food for insects and their young. Insects also feed on leaf litter on the ground, decomposing it and turning it into a rich mixture of nutrients. Butterflies and bees visit flowers to drink nectar. As they feed, bees also carry pollen from one flower to another, helping the flowers to reproduce. Birds and mammals also help in plant reproduction by feeding on fruits and discarding the seeds on the ground.

Below ground, worms feed on the soil, mixing and breaking it down. Predators such as moles dig through the soil after them with their powerful feet. Ants leave their nest chambers to search for food on the surface.

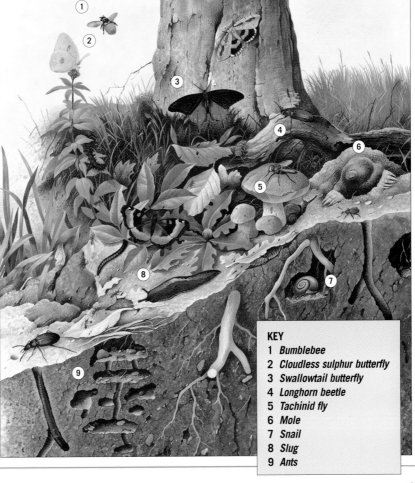

KEY
1 *Bumblebee*
2 *Cloudless sulphur butterfly*
3 *Swallowtail butterfly*
4 *Longhorn beetle*
5 *Tachinid fly*
6 *Mole*
7 *Snail*
8 *Slug*
9 *Ants*

RIVER LIFE

RIVERS hold a very small proportion of the earth's water, but they are extremely important habitats for many kinds of animals. At their source, usually in the mountains, rivers are fast-flowing, and plants cannot root themselves in the river bed. The main source of food for invertebrates, such as water-living snails, leeches, and fly larvae, is decaying plant material. This is washed downstream from vegetation that overhangs the river, and is filtered from the water by the invertebrates as they cling to the rocky river bed. Birds and strong-swimming fish then feed on the invertebrates.

Further downstream, as the gradient lessens, a river is slower-moving. The mud and silt that collect on the river bottom form a bed for plants to take root. Worms and snails burrow into the mud, while insects and their larvae feed on the plants and the algae that grow on them. They in turn become prey for fish and frogs. Plants also provide protection from predators for newly hatched fish, amphibians, and insects.

This slow-moving river in Europe *(below)*, is thronged with life. Dragonflies hunt smaller insects above the surface, while herons and otters hunt for fish.

KEY

1 *Kingfisher*	12 *Great crested newt*
2 *Otter*	
3 *Reed warbler*	13 *Water scorpion*
4 *Mayfly*	
5 *Dragonfly*	14 *Toad spawn*
6 *Damselfly*	15 *Perch*
7 *Moorhen*	16 *Pond snail*
8 *Water vole*	17 *Great diving beetle*
9 *Heron*	
10 *Frog*	18 *Stickleback*
11 *Water boatman*	19 *Crayfish*

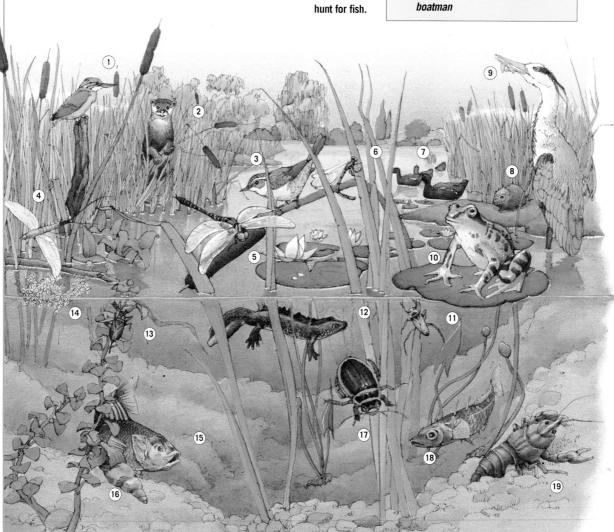

Salmon are born in rivers, then swim out to the sea. They return to the rivers to lay their eggs, swimming and leaping upstream against the current.

PONDS AND LAKES

The still, calm waters of ponds and lakes are an ideal habitat for microscopic floating plants known as algae. They are fed upon by tiny animals, called zooplankton, which are then eaten by insects, snails, and small fish.

The great diving beetle lives in ponds. It grabs its prey, even small fish, with its front legs.

The many kinds of fish found in slow-moving waters are a vital source of food for large predators. Large fish, such as the pike in Europe, patrol the waters in search of smaller fish to eat. Turtles and swift-moving otters also swim in search of fish. Birds skim insects from the surface, and dive or wade through the water, stabbing with their beaks to make their catch.

The river banks provide shelter for many animals. Small mammals such as voles live in holes above the water line, while birds nest among the tall reeds and rushes that often grow in the shallows.

In small ponds, the major predators are newts and frogs, while fish can be found in larger ponds and lakes. Tall water plants take root in the bottom. They provide insect larvae with a "ladder" out of the water when they emerge to become adults.

Wetlands are formed at the edges of lakes, where rivers meet the sea, or where the land is flooded. Potentially highly fertile, wetlands are one of our most threatened habitats, as they are often reclaimed for farming or for building land.

The Everglades of Florida, in the United States *(right)*, is an area of swampland and slow-moving water. Tall reeds dominate the waterlogged land. Wading birds such as flamingoes and spoonbills feed in the shallows, while alligators roam the deeper water.

KEY
1 *Everglade kite*
2 *Flamingo*
3 *Alligator*
4 *Spoonbill*
5 *Swamp rabbit*
6 *Cottonmouth*
7 *Raccoon*
8 *Tree frog*
9 *Tarpon (young fish)*

KEY
1 *Yak*
2 *Snow leopard*
3 *Himalayan ibex*
4 *Pika*

The peaks of the Himalayan mountain range, in southern central Asia, are rocky and snow-covered. The highest ridges are the territory of sure-footed animals such as the Himalayan ibex. The ibex is the favorite prey of the powerful snow leopard, whose white coat camouflages it against the snow. Its coat is thick, and even its paws are covered with fur to keep out the cold. Pikas, small relatives of rabbits, can also fall victim to the snow leopard if they are not agile and fast enough to escape.

The largest animal in the Himalayas, the yak, also has thick fur, with another coat of long hair on top. This keeps the yaks so warm that they have to move higher up the mountains to cooler areas in the summer.

MOUNTAINS

THE HIGHEST mountaintops are covered with snow all year round. Those that lie in tropical regions, such as Kilimanjaro in Africa, can have hot, steamy rain forest at their foothills and freezing nighttime temperatures at their summits. At high altitudes the sunlight is intense. There are strong, cold winds and a lack of oxygen in the air.

Despite these dangers, mountains can host a wide variety of life. Both animals and plants have adapted to live in such harsh conditions. On tropical mountains, some species of plants and animals have developed in isolation. The plants are not able to spread their seeds far enough to reach another mountain, and even the animals cannot migrate from one mountain to another, because of the inhospitable heat in the lowlands.

On their lower slopes, mountains are often forested, but higher up the trees give way to dry scrubland and rocky, windswept terrain. The flowering plants that grow here are short and strong, and are able to conserve water as much as possible in the drying winds. Close to the summit, only the most hardy kinds of plants, such as lichens and mosses, can grow. With the coming of spring, snow covering much of the mountain may melt and new plants emerge.

Insects abound on the mountains during the warmer summer months, but many are flightless, as they would be swept away by the strong winds. Even in the snow-covered high peaks, insects and spiders survive. They feed on frozen insects that are blown up from the lowlands by the winds.

Small mammals such as the pika in Asia, or the rock hyrax in Africa, live in burrows or rocky outcrops, to protect themselves from the worst of the cold and wind. Many also hibernate during the winter. Larger animals have thick fur or woolly coats to keep out the cold. Grazing animals, such as sheep and goats, live at the highest altitudes. Their nimble hooves are able to negotiate even the most treacherous slopes. They are preyed upon by wolves, snow leopards, and cougars or mountain lions.

Only the strongest-flying birds, such as eagles and other birds of prey, are able to withstand the winds around the mountain summits. They soar on currents of air, swooping down to catch rodents and other small mammals.

High above the Andes mountain range in South America, the Andean condor *(above)*, one of the biggest birds in the world, soars for many miles without flapping its wings. As it soars, it searches for carrion, its principal diet. In between the summits are high, grassy plateaux, where guanacos *(below)*, wild relatives of the llama, roam.

ARCTIC

MUCH OF THE Arctic Ocean is covered with a thick layer of floating ice all year round. At its edges, rafts of broken ice, called pack ice, drift in the freezing cold waters. During the summer, some of the ice cracks and melts, forming waterways and large stretches of water.

No plants can grow on the Arctic ice, so most life is found in the waters around it. During the summer, the days become longer, and the sun warms the waters. Phytoplankton, tiny plant material that floats in the water, quickly grows and multiplies in these conditions, providing food for millions of tiny animals called zooplankton.

With the sudden increase in zooplankton, many animals migrate to the Arctic during the summer to exploit this rich source of food. Fish, squid, birds, and even giant whales feed on the zooplankton. A shrimp-like kind called krill is a particular favorite. Seals hunt the fish, while walruses search for shellfish and crabs on the sea bed with their sensitive whiskers. The largest predators in the waters are killer whales, which feed on fish and seals, while on the ice the huge polar bear roams. Its white coat is perfect camouflage while it waits to grab a seal as it emerges from a hole in the ice to breathe.

KEY
1 *Arctic tern*
2 *Polar bear*
3 *Bearded seal*
4 *Narwhal*
5 *Walrus*

In winter, most of the ocean freezes over again, and the days are short and dark. Without sunshine to make food, phytoplankton cannot grow. Zooplankton sink into the depths of the ocean, where they feed on one another, or off fat reserves stored during the summer. Most of the larger animals migrate south to find new sources of food. Polar bears are among the few animals that remain. Some roam the ice or nearby land during the winter, while others dig dens in the snow to shelter from the harsh weather until the spring. Here females give birth to their cubs.

NORTH AMERICA

ARCTIC OCEAN

North Pole

ASIA

EUROPE

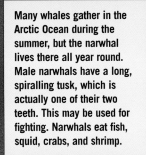

Many whales gather in the Arctic Ocean during the summer, but the narwhal lives there all year round. Male narwhals have a long, spiralling tusk, which is actually one of their two teeth. This may be used for fighting. Narwhals eat fish, squid, crabs, and shrimp.

TUNDRA

THE LAND that borders the Arctic Ocean is treeless, and the soil is permanently frozen. For most of the year, this region, known as tundra, is a barren wilderness, where plant and animal life is scarce. During the short summer, however, the ice on the top layer of the ground melts, and small plants can grow.

Herds of caribou or reindeer (*above*, 1) arrive from the taiga forests to the south to feed on the new growth. The melted ice forms boggy patches where insects thrive, providing food for migrant birds. Small mammals such as lemmings (2), that have spent the winter beneath the snow, are preyed upon by Arctic foxes and owls (3).

ANTARCTICA

THE CONTINENT of Antarctica is a huge, mountainous landmass, much of it covered by a permanent ice cap almost 2 miles (3.2 km) thick in some places. It is the coldest place in the world. In winter, the ocean waters that surround the continent are covered with floating pack ice and icebergs that have broken off the edges of the coastal ice shelf. Bitter winds sweep up snow from the ground into fierce blizzards.

The only places where plants can grow on this barren land are along the coasts and around the Antarctic Peninsula. Even then, they are mostly tiny mosses and lichens growing on the rocks. There is not enough food on the land to feed anything larger than small insects, so the animals of Antarctica are clustered around the coasts and islands, where the ocean waters provide them with plenty of food.

In summer, humpback whales migrate thousands of miles from their tropical breeding grounds to feed in the Antarctic.

The ice cap extends across Antarctica. There are only a few small areas where the ice melts enough for plants to grow. No people live there permanently, although explorers and scientists visit. At the edge of the coastal ice shelf, colonies of penguins gather (below), feeding on fish in the cold waters.

Just as in the Arctic, the main source of food for many animals is plankton. Phytoplankton and zooplankton (see page 30) thrive in the Antarctic, due to nutrient-rich currents and upwellings that swirl through the cold waters. Fish throng the waters, feeding on the zooplankton. Whales also migrate to the Antarctic to feed on vast quantities of krill. Despite its name, the crabeater seal also feeds almost entirely on krill—the only seal to do so.

Other seals and penguins dive after fish, while sea birds such as albatrosses and terns pluck the fish from the surface. Penguins and seals come out onto land to breed or rest, but when they return to the water, they are in danger from hunting killer whales and the ferocious leopard seal.

Antarctica is home to several kinds of penguins. They spend most of their lives at sea, coming ashore to breed in large colonies on the ice. Emperor penguins are the largest. After their eggs are laid, the females return to the sea to feed. The males look after the eggs, carrying them on their feet to keep them off the ice. In the coldest weather, they huddle together in circular groups. Six weeks later, the chicks hatch, the mothers return, and the fathers can finally feed.

Adélie penguins are the favorite food of the leopard seal, which will also eat young seals, even of its own kind. Adélie penguins are so fearful of this hunter that they hesitate at the water's edge, none daring to be first to take the plunge.

Antarctic animals are specially adapted to survive the cold, icy conditions and winds of up to 124 miles (200 km) per hour. They have thick fur or feathers, and many also have a layer of fat, called blubber, to keep them warm. Some insects can survive being frozen during winter and defrosted in summer, while some kinds of fish have a natural "antifreeze" in their blood to stop them freezing in the icy waters.

OCEANS

THE OCEANS cover more than 139 million square miles (360 million km²) of the earth's surface, approximately 71% of its total area. More than 317 cubic miles (1350 million km³) of water is contained within it, representing 97% of the earth's entire supply. The oceans hold enough salt in them to cover Europe to a depth of 3.1 miles (5 km). There are four great oceans: in order of size, the Pacific, Atlantic, Indian, and Arctic Oceans.

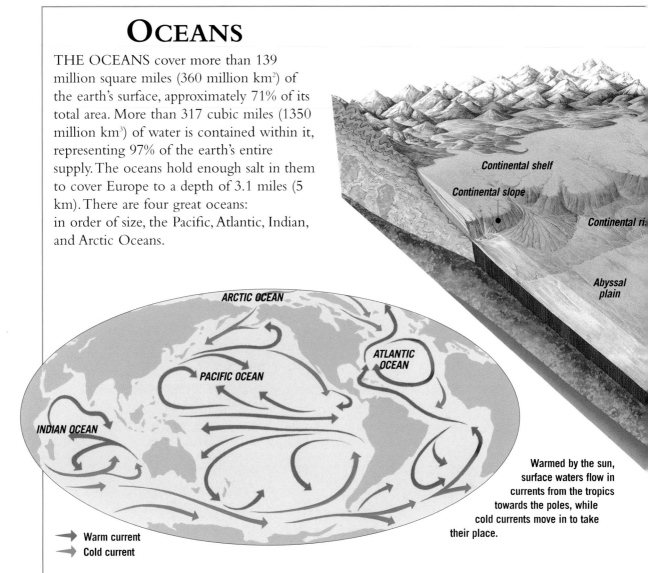

Continental shelf

Continental slope

Continental ri[

Abyssal plain

ARCTIC OCEAN

ATLANTIC OCEAN

PACIFIC OCEAN

INDIAN OCEAN

Warmed by the sun, surface waters flow in currents from the tropics towards the poles, while cold currents move in to take their place.

→ Warm current
→ Cold current

The ocean waters are not still, but move in tides and currents. Tides shift the water daily under the gravitational pull of the moon *(see page 51)*. Currents, great flowing bands of water, swirl around the globe. There are two kinds: surface currents, which are swept along by the wind, and deepwater currents, which are generated by differences in density (the colder and saltier the water is, the greater its density).

In the open oceans, currents flow clockwise in the northern hemisphere, counterclockwise in the southern. This is the Coriolis effect, caused by the direction of rotation of the planet. Ocean currents have a great influence on climate. The warm Gulf Stream, for example, brings relatively mild winters to northwestern Europe.

Only about 20% of the earth's species live in the oceans, of which about 90% are bottom-living, shallow-water species. In most ocean waters, especially the zone below a depth of 3,000 feet (914 m) where no light penetrates, life is extremely sparse.

There are two main ocean habitats: the water itself, or pelagic habitat, and the ocean floor, called the benthic habitat. Both habitats are subdivided into several zones, according to the amount of sunlight that is able to reach down through the water. Most life is concentrated in the upper 650 feet (200 m) where tiny plants and animals called plankton congregate, providing a rich source of food. But some animals survive in the dark, near-freezing waters more than 2.5 miles (4000 m) down.

THE OCEAN FLOOR

The ocean floor is mostly a level plain, but it also features mountain ranges, volcanic peaks, long ridges, deep trenches, and high ledges where it borders the continents.

The flat plain that forms most of the ocean is called the abyssal plain. It lies at an average depth of about 3 miles (4,828 m) and is covered by a thick layer of sediment called ooze. This consists of mud and gravel—and billions of skeletons of dead animals that have collected at the bottom. The continental shelf, the ledge that surrounds the abyssal plain, plunges relatively steeply down to it at the continental slope. The water above the continental shelf, really a part of the continent that lies under the ocean, is never deeper than 650 feet (198 m). It is here that most ocean life is found.

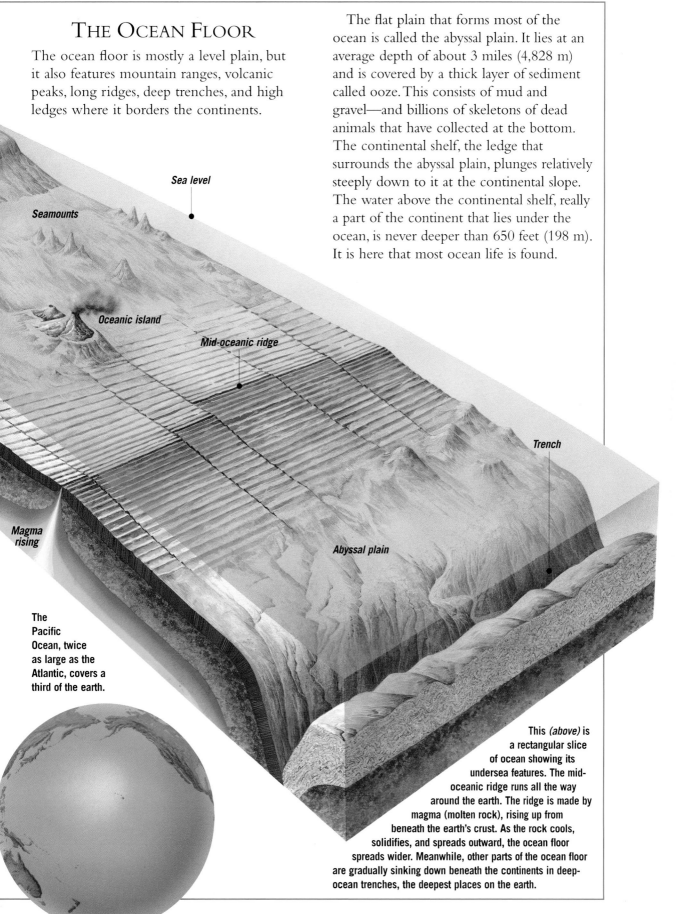

Sea level

Seamounts

Oceanic island

Mid-oceanic ridge

Trench

Magma rising

Abyssal plain

The Pacific Ocean, twice as large as the Atlantic, covers a third of the earth.

This *(above)* is a rectangular slice of ocean showing its undersea features. The mid-oceanic ridge runs all the way around the earth. The ridge is made by magma (molten rock), rising up from beneath the earth's crust. As the rock cools, solidifies, and spreads outward, the ocean floor spreads wider. Meanwhile, other parts of the ocean floor are gradually sinking down beneath the continents in deep-ocean trenches, the deepest places on the earth.

SURFACE WATERS

THE RICHEST VARIETY of life in the oceans is found in the surface waters. Here, light from the sun penetrates the water, allowing plants to grow. Unlike land plants, oceanic plants cannot put down roots into the ground. Instead, they drift through the water in the form of tiny, usually single-celled organisms, known as phytoplankton. They use sunlight and nutrients dissolved in the water to make food by the process of photosynthesis.

Phytoplankton comprise most of the plant material found in the oceans (a small amount also comes from seaweeds and shallow-water marine grasses). Able to grow very quickly, they are the first and vital stage in the food web of the oceans.

Phytoplankton are fed upon by tiny animals called zooplankton. These include the larvae (young) of fish, as well as tiny relatives of crabs and shrimps, known as copepods. They rise and fall through the water, using the surface currents to carry them along to new grazing areas. Plankton is richest in those parts of the ocean where nutrients are stirred up from the ocean floor by currents or winds, such as

Phytoplankton *(above left),* and the larger zooplankton *(above right)* that feed on them.

on the continental shelf *(see page 34).* In some oceans, the amount of plankton in the water peaks in the spring and autumn. Many plankton-eating animals breed or migrate to coincide with these peaks.

Zooplankton provide food for a wide range of ocean animals. In an attempt to escape attention, many zooplankton have confusing color patterns, and some are even transparent. Fish and squid are major predators of zooplankton, and shoals of small fish throng the surface waters. They in turn attract larger predators. The Portuguese man-of-war floats on the surface, trailing its stinging tentacles down to catch small fish.

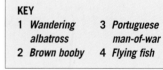

KEY
1 *Wandering albatross*
2 *Brown booby*
3 *Portuguese man-of-war*
4 *Flying fish*

Sea birds *(see illustration, opposite)* glide over the ocean waves, looking out for fish. Some birds scoop up fish from the surface with their beaks or feet, while others, such as the booby, dive right into the water to grab their prey. Below the surface, small fish are preyed upon by larger, fast-moving predatory fish, such as tuna or sharks. They also fall prey to sea turtles, and mammals such as seals, dolphins, and whales. With so many different predators, many fish have evolved patterns of color for camouflage, or spiny or armored skin, for protection.

The surface waters are home to some of the largest animals in the world. Many of these, however, feed on the smallest creatures of all, zooplankton. Baleen whales, such as the blue whale or the sei whale, as well as some sharks like the basking shark, take in great mouthfuls of water and filter out vast quantities of a shrimplike zooplankton called krill.

KEY
1 *Anchovies*
2 *Tarpon*
3 *Blue marlin*
4 *Squid*
5 *Hawksbill turtle*
6 *Manta ray*
7 *Skipjack tuna*
8 *Sei whale*
9 *Dolphinfish*

The surface waters contain the most abundant food supply in the oceans.

37

CORAL REEFS

CORAL is found in tropical shallow waters around volcanic islands or close to rocky mainland coastlines. It is made from layers of the skeletons of tiny animals called polyps. Over many years, colonies of polyps can build up great banks of coral, known as reefs. There are many different kinds of corals, and their bright colors make a coral reef look like an undersea garden. Only the living surface of the coral is colored—the layers of dead polyps underneath are white. The living layer of tiny polyps feed on zooplankton *(see page 36)* that drifts by in the current.

Coral reefs are crowded with animal life. Tiny plants called algae, which drift in the current or live on the bodies of the coral, are food for zooplankton, as well as for larger animals such as fish and sea urchins. The crown-of-thorns starfish and the parrotfish feed on the coral itself. Many kinds of brightly colored fish throng the reef. Some feed on plankton, shellfish, and other small creatures. Others, including the largest predators such as sharks, eels, and barracudas, hunt smaller fish.

As fish, starfish and sea urchins feed on algae growing on corals, they break off pieces of dead coral. These form the sandy beaches often found on coral reefs.

Some corals are branched, others mound-shaped. Some look like colorful flowers.

KEY		
1 Nautilus	13 Angelfish	25 Sweetlips
2 Squid	14 Butterflyfish	26 Trumpetfish
3 Trunkfish	15 Starfish	27 Damselfish
4 Surgeonfish	16 Porcupinefish	28 Butterflyfish
5 Triggerfish	17 Seahorse	29 Jellyfish
6 Seahorse	18 Wrasse	30 Tube sponge
7 Moray eel	19 Grouper	31 Clownfish
8 Hatchetfish	20 Surgeonfish	
9 Starfish	21 Sea anemones	
10 Angelfish	22 Coral hind	
11 Octopus	23 Angelfish	
12 Moorish idol	24 Butterflyfish	

The coral reef provides places to hide for predators and prey. The moray eel shoots out of a hole to grab passing fish. Clownfish hide among the stinging tentacles of sea anemones. Other fish would be killed, but they remain unharmed.

Between 650 feet (198 m) and 3,300 feet (1,006 m) deep, there is an area of water known as the twilight zone. Hatchetfish, lanternfish, and the deadly siphonophore, a kind of jellyfish, migrate up toward the surface to feed. Barracudinas prey on any fish they can find, their stomachs expanding to take large prey. The viperfish has a glowing rod on its back to attract prey toward its mouth.

KEY
1 *Siphonophore*   4 *Viperfish*   6 *Lanternfish*
2 *Loosejaw*   5 *Barracudinas* 7 *Hatchetfish*
3 *Argentine*

The six-gilled shark has six gill openings instead of the normal five. Preferring the cold waters of the deep, it feeds on fish and rays near the ocean floor.

DEEPWATER LIFE

LIGHT CANNOT penetrate very far through water, so after a depth of about 650 feet (198 m) there is little light, and below 3,300 feet (1,006 m) the water is completely black and very cold. Phytoplankton cannot survive here, and the amount of animal life is greatly reduced. As there is no source of plant material to feed on, any creatures living in the deep waters need to find alternative sources of food.

Some scavenging deepwater animals feed on the dead plant and animal matter that rains down through the water from the surface waters above. Others, such as the hatchetfish, travel up toward the surface to feed, then return to the depths. On the way, they must avoid falling victim to the many predatory deepwater animals that patrol the dark waters.

Animals that live in the deep waters all the time need to be specially adapted to survive. They are mostly small, and their bodies are frail and lacking in muscle mass. These factors reduce the amount of energy, and therefore food, needed to maintain their bodies. They have large, extremely sensitive eyes to see in the near-black waters. Many are colored brown or black for camouflage, to conceal themselves from predators. Some prawns are bright red, but this color is invisible at such depths.

Predators must adapt to an even greater extent in an environment where prey is scarce, and where there may be long periods of time between each successful attack. Fish such as the viperfish have long jaws and extremely long, needle-sharp teeth, which are backward-pointing for stabbing and holding on to their prey. To take advantage of any prey animal they encounter, many predators, such as the gulper eel, have huge jaws and stomachs that can stretch to hold fish even larger than themselves.

Despite the blackness of the water, there is still some light in the depths of the ocean. Some deepwater animals are able to produce light from their own bodies, either from their tissues or from special light-producing organs. This feature is known as bioluminescence. These lights may act as a lure to prey animals, or as a signal to others of the same species in the search for mates. They may also be "flashed" on and off to confuse an attacker.

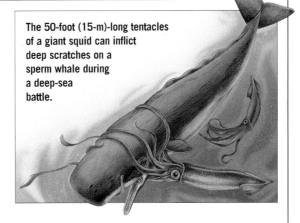

The 50-foot (15-m)-long tentacles of a giant squid can inflict deep scratches on a sperm whale during a deep-sea battle.

As well as the small predators that live in the deep, larger animals also visit deep waters to hunt for prey. Deep-living sharks and deep-diving whales feed on fish and squid. Although whales need to come to the surface to breathe, some are able to stay underwater for long periods of time. The sperm whale may dive to 2 miles (3,219 m) below the surface, and stay there for up to two hours in search of its favorite prey, giant squid.

KEY
1 *Vampire squid*
2 *Anglerfish*
3 *Gulper eels*
4 *Anglerfish*
5 *Prawns*

Many of the animals that live in the deepwater zone look quite terrifying—apart from their small size. The glowing "lamp" hanging from the head of the anglerfish family attracts smaller fish which mistake it for prey, only to be snapped up themselves. Some anglerfish have teeth that lie flat and then spring back around their prey when it is inside their mouths. The gulper eel conserves energy by lying in wait and ambushing its prey.

OCEAN FLOOR

AT THE LEVEL of the ocean floor, about 15,000 feet (4,572 m) deep, the water is completely black, and very cold. Animals living there cannot use sight to find their food—in fact, many are blind. Instead, they have highly developed senses of touch, or are able to detect chemical changes in the water that lead them to a food source.

The floor of the oceans is covered with a thick layer of ooze, made up of sand, mud and, tiny particles of rock, as well as debris from plant and animal life in the waters above. Some animals feed on this debris by burrowing into the ooze or creeping across it. Their digestive systems are specially adapted to process a diet of animal remains, including skeletons and droppings.

With their bases rooted in the ooze and their tentacles waving in the water, sea pens, relatives of corals and sea anemones, look almost like plants. Sponges such as the Venus flower basket also bed themselves into the ooze, filtering out debris from the water. Spiky-skinned sea urchins and their relatives, the sea cucumbers, have branched tentacles, known as tube-feet, beneath their bodies. Some of these help them to move across or burrow into the ooze, while others gather food from the water or the ocean floor, and pass it to the mouth.

As well as the scavengers, predatory animals are also found on the ocean floor. Sea spiders pick their way across the floor, their very long legs keeping them out of the soft ooze. They feed on sponges and burrowing worms.

Only a few kinds of fish are found close to the ocean floor. Among these is the rat-tail, which has a large head and a long body which tapers into an even longer tail. It makes a loud drumming noise by vibrating muscles attached to its swim bladder (the organ that keeps it afloat). This may be a way of signaling to others of its kind.

The tripod fish, as its name suggests, holds itself off the ocean floor on a "tripod" made of its long, stiltlike fins and tail. It sinks the tips of its fins into the soft surface of the ooze, to support its body. Another pair of fins is held up in the air to detect the movements of passing prey, whereupon the tripod fish pushes itself forward to feed.

The ocean floor is littered with human waste, including old fishing nets, cans and bottles, and wrecks of sunken ships. Found on all parts of the ocean floor, especially beneath major shipping lanes, is clinker, burnt coal dumped from steamships during the period between the 1850s and 1950s.

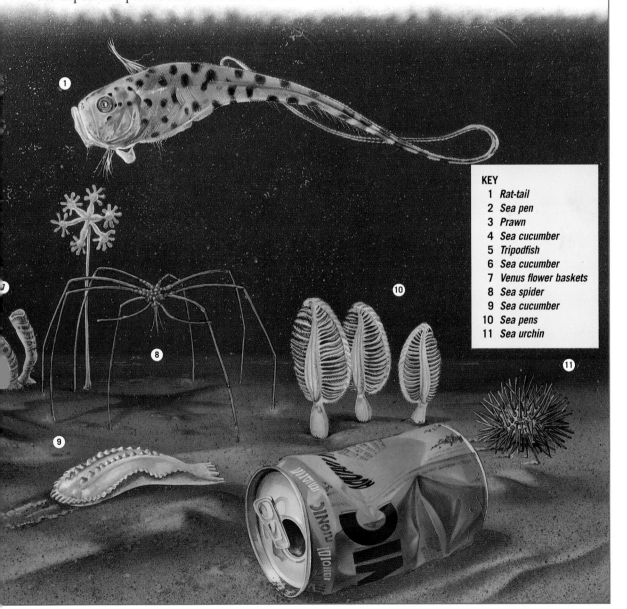

KEY
1 *Rat-tail*
2 *Sea pen*
3 *Prawn*
4 *Sea cucumber*
5 *Tripodfish*
6 *Sea cucumber*
7 *Venus flower baskets*
8 *Sea spider*
9 *Sea cucumber*
10 *Sea pens*
11 *Sea urchin*

BLACK SMOKERS

SNAKING ACROSS the ocean floor are undersea mountain chains known as mid-oceanic ridges. Here, the earth's crust is gradually spreading apart and magma, hot molten rock from beneath the crust, rises to the surface of the sea bed. In some places along a mid-oceanic ridge, water seeping down into the rocks is heated by the magma. It shoots up through cracks in the ocean floor, known as hydrothermal vents.

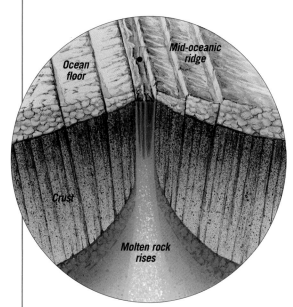

As magma rises, it spreads apart the old rocks of the ocean floor. It then solidifies, forming a new part of the ocean floor.

These jets of water are rich in minerals from the earth's crust, especially sulfur. As the minerals emerge, they are gradually deposited around the vents, creating tall chimneys. The sulfur turns the waters around the vents black, and gives these chimneys their name: "black smokers."

Most of the deep-sea ocean floor is very cold, with little animal life to be found. The temperature of the water shooting out of the black smokers, however, can be higher than 572°F (300°C). In the warm, mineral-rich water close by, an amazing amount of life flourishes. Some creatures are found nowhere else in the world, and several kinds reach enormous sizes.

Among the most peculiar animals are tube worms. These 10-foot (3-m)-long worms cluster together in intertwined masses, most of their red bodies hidden inside white tube shells. Giant clams also thrive around the black smokers, while white, eyeless crabs and lobsters scavenge for scraps of food stirred up by the warm, swirling waters. Even a few kinds of fish live here, including the eelpout and members of a group of long-bodied fish called brotulids, which prefer to live in dark places.

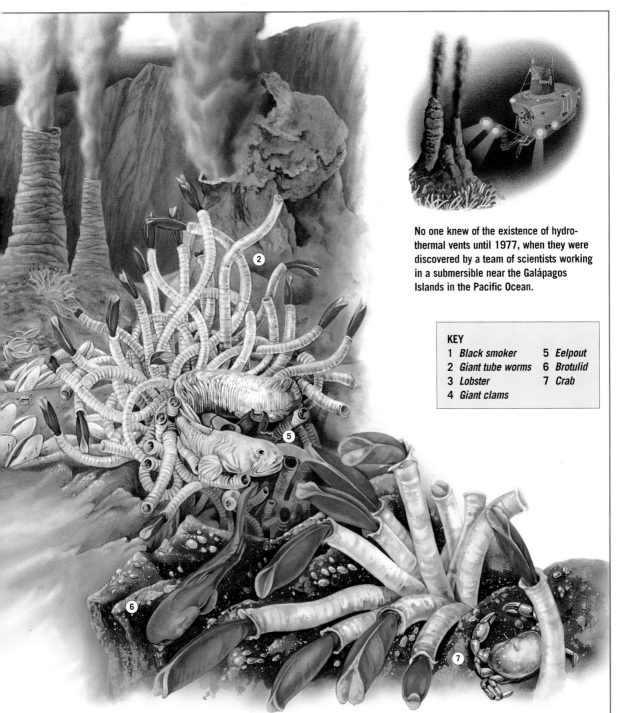

No one knew of the existence of hydro-thermal vents until 1977, when they were discovered by a team of scientists working in a submersible near the Galápagos Islands in the Pacific Ocean.

KEY

1	*Black smoker*	5	*Eelpout*
2	*Giant tube worms*	6	*Brotulid*
3	*Lobster*	7	*Crab*
4	*Giant clams*		

Without sunlight to grow plants, life around the black smokers relies on bacteria, which convert the sulfur dissolved in the water into food. This process is known as chemosynthesis. The bacteria provide food for some animals, which are then prey for predators. Tube worms and giant clams actually have bacteria inside their bodies to make food for them, as they do not have mouthparts or guts to feed themselves.

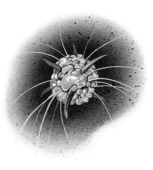

A small creature looking a little like a dandelion is also found near the black smokers. A kind of siphonophore *(see page 40)* related to the jellyfish, this animal holds itself above the sea bed with fine tentacles. Other tentacles, armed with stinging cells, capture its prey.

OCEAN TRENCHES

THE DEEPEST places on the earth, ocean trenches are formed when the huge plates that make up the earth's surface push together, forcing one to slide beneath the other. This creates great chasms in the ocean floor that can plunge down to 6 miles (9,656 m) deep. At such depths, the water pressure is crushing, and the movement of the ocean floor creates frequent underwater earthquakes. Incredibly, there are some animals that can survive even here.

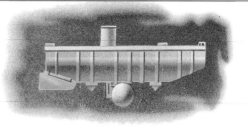

In 1960, scientists descended 6.78 miles (10,911 m) into the Marianas Trench in the Pacific Ocean, in the submersible *Trieste*.

Sea cucumbers *(see page 42)* creep across the ooze that gathers at the bottom of the trench. Worms and sea anemones burrow into the sand to avoid predators such as brotulid fish, the world's deepest-living fish. These animals are specially adapted to live in such a high-pressure environment. Their bodies have no air spaces inside them, and they would die if they were brought up into shallower, lower-pressure waters.

Ocean trenches are so black, cold, and hostile that scientists have named them the "hadal zone" after Hades, the Greek god of the underworld.

KEY
1 *Brotulid*
2 *Sea anemone*
3 *Sea cucumber*
4 *Polychaete worm*

Modern submersibles can travel to the deepest parts of the oceans. The scientists inside breathe air that is stored on board, and can direct the submersible through the water. Submersibles have strong searchlights, as the waters are pitch black below about 3,300 feet (1,006 m). They have cameras for the scientists to take photographs or video footage. Some of the most fascinating parts of the ocean, such as hydrothermal vents *(see page 44),* were discovered by scientists in submersibles. Deep-sea creatures never seen before have also been photographed and identified.

OCEAN EXPLORATION

IN ORDER to explore the vast areas below the surface of the oceans, humans need to be able to travel to great depths without having to return to the surface every few minutes to breathe. Nineteenth-century divers wore heavy suits and dome-like helmets, with pipes leading up to the surface through which air was pumped. The invention of the scuba diving system, where air was carried in a tank on the diver's back, gave divers much more freedom.

However, below about 164 feet (50 m),

water pressure makes the air in the tanks too concentrated. Divers who want to go deeper into the oceans have to breathe a different mixture of gases. After diving in deep, high-pressure waters, they enter a diving bell to return to surface pressure before they move up through the water. This stops nitrogen bubbles building up inside their blood, giving them the "bends."

At greater depths, divers use underwater vehicles called submersibles, which have thick metal walls to withstand the pressure of the water. Robot vehicles controlled from the surface, with cameras and sample-gathering equipment, are also used.

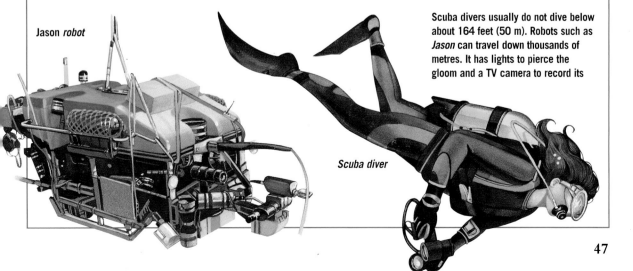

Jason *robot*

Scuba diver

Scuba divers usually do not dive below about 164 feet (50 m). Robots such as *Jason* can travel down thousands of metres. It has lights to pierce the gloom and a TV camera to record its

OCEAN GIANTS

SOME OF the largest animals in the world live in the oceans. They can grow so large because the water supports their huge bodies. On land, even air-breathing mammals such as whales would die, collapsed under their own weight. They can also grow to enormous sizes because of the abundance of food in the oceans. The vast quantities of plant and animal plankton *(see pages 36-37)* support all ocean life, either by providing food for small animals that are then eaten by larger ones, or by feeding the large animals directly.

In fact, some of the largest whales and sharks in the oceans feed only on tiny zooplankton such as krill, which are only 2 inches (5 cm) long. The 98-foot (30-m)-long blue whale eats 4.4 tons (4 tonnes) of krill every day, but because krill reproduce very quickly, they remain abundant. Blue whales and other plankton-eaters migrate to the polar regions during the summer. They feed on the high densities of plant and animal plankton that build up due to the rise in temperature and long hours of sunlight.

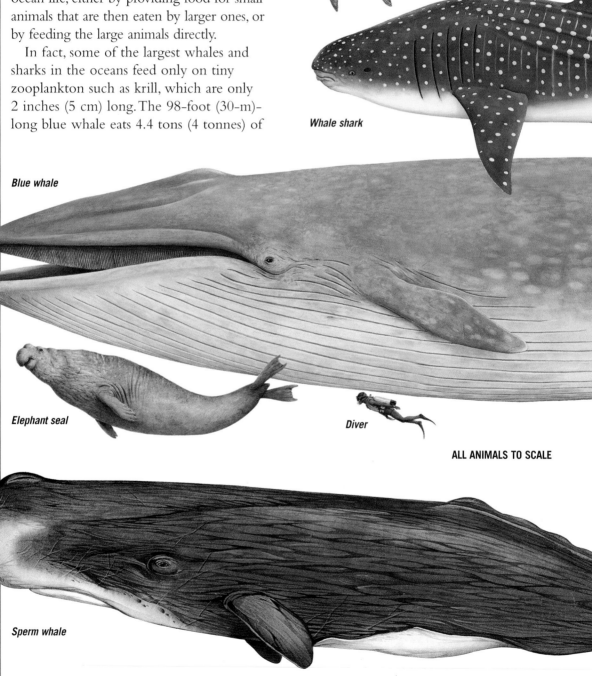

Leatherback turtle

Whale shark

Blue whale

Elephant seal

Diver

ALL ANIMALS TO SCALE

Sperm whale

The 49-mile (15-m)-long whale shark and the 20-foot (6-m)-wide manta ray also feed on plankton, as well as on tiny fish. Unlike the blue whale, which filters plankton from the water through the horny plates in its mouth, these giants filter plankton through their gill slits. The whale shark has many teeth, but they are tiny and useless.

Pacific octopus

Other ocean giants are predators of larger fish and other animals. The leatherback turtle, almost 6.5 feet (2 m) in length, dives a half mile (900 m) or more in search of jellyfish to eat. The Pacific octopus lives on the ocean floor. It grabs crabs and lobsters with its long arms, which can span 30 feet (9 m).

Elephant seals feed on fish and squid. The males can weigh over 2.2 tons (2 tonnes), three times as much as the females. The 59-foot (18-m)-long sperm whale hunts deep-living giant squid *(see page 41)*. Its huge head takes up one third of its whole length, and contains a waxy substance that helps it to sink and rise through the water.

Some of the most fearsome hunters in the oceans are the predatory sharks. The great white shark is usually about 23 feet (7 m) long. It feeds on sea mammals such as seals and, despite its reputation, may often only attack humans by mistake.

Manta ray

Great white shark

The giant squid is the longest invertebrate (animal without a backbone). Including its 10 long, sucker- and hook-covered arms, it can measure 66 feet (20 m) in length. No live specimen has ever been seen.

Giant squid

KEY
1 Common tern
2 Black-headed gull
3 Herring gull
4 Oystercatcher
5 Limpets
6 Mussels
7 Periwinkle
8 Barnacles
9 Shore crab
10 Prawn
11 Bladder wrack
   (seaweed)
12 Sea lettuce
13 Starfish
14 Stickleback
15 Hermit crab
16 Blenny
17 Sea anemone
18 Whelk

SEASHORE

THE SEASHORE is the place where the land meets the sea. It can consist of rocky cliffs, a sandy beach, or mudflats bordering a river mouth or estuary. The animals and plants that live there must be able to survive the tides that cover them in salt water at certain times of the day, and leave them exposed to the air at other times. They live at different levels on the seashore according to how well they can survive out of water.

Many kinds of seaweed dry out easily, and are found low down on the shore where they are covered with water all the time. Other more hardy varieties live further up the shore. They anchor themselves to rocks to stop themselves being pulled away at high tide, and are covered with mucus to hold in moisture when the tide goes out.

Animals that live on sandy or muddy shores burrow into the ground at low tide to keep moist and cool. On rocky shores, mussels clamp their shells tightly together, while limpets attach themselves to wet rocks to stop themselves drying out. This also prevents them from being pulled away by powerful waves when the tide comes back in. On some shores, tidal pools form between rocks. These are rich in life, including animals such as starfish, sea anemones, and small fish, which could not otherwise survive so far up the shore.

Whelks, snails, and slugs move about on one large foot. They are known as gastropods.

In rock pools *(above),* algae growing on the rocks are eaten by limpets, snails, and periwinkles, which are themselves prey for starfish and whelks. Seaweeds are also a source of food, as well as a cool, damp shelter when the tide goes out. Crabs such as the hermit crab, which takes over the shell of a dead animal, scavenge on animal debris. Birds such as oystercatchers and gulls probe the pools and shore for worms, fish, and shelled animals.

Every day, sea levels rise and fall in the movement of the tides. Tides are caused by the pull of the moon's gravity on the earth. As the earth rotates, the ocean waters on the side of the earth closest to the moon (and the opposite side) are pulled into a bulge, causing a high tide *(right).* The rest of the earth has a low tide. When the sun and moon are in line, the sun's gravity increases the pull to give extra-high and extra-low tides *(far right).*

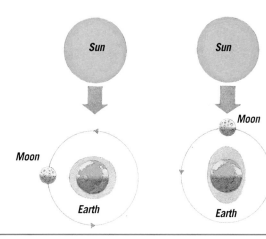

ISLAND LIFE

CUT OFF FROM the continental land masses by stretches of ocean water, islands often have a range of plant and animal life that is uniquely their own. Some islands were once part of a larger land mass, while others are formed by underwater volcanoes. As soon as an island forms, it begins to be colonized by plants and animals. Islands close to the mainland are colonized more quickly than remote ones.

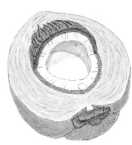

The coconut palm is one of the few trees that can disperse their seeds over long distances. The large coconuts have a waterproof outer coating that allows them to float for thousands of miles to remote islands.

Plant seeds can travel across the oceans. They rely on the wind or water to carry them to islands. Seeds can also be carried in the fur or feathers of animals, or even in their digestive systems. The light seeds of small plants can travel further on the winds than those of large trees, so there are sometimes few, if any, trees on the most remote islands. But these small plants may, over many years, evolve into larger ones.

The blue-footed booby *(left)*, nests on the steep cliff faces of the Galápagos Islands, off the coast of South America. It plunges into the water to feed on fish and squid. The male and female take turns sitting on their eggs.

The only lizards to feed in the sea, marine iguanas *(below)* are also found in the Galápagos Islands. They bask in the sun to warm up before diving into the water to graze on seaweed and algae 50 feet (15.2 m) below the surface.

Birds and swimming animals such as seals are often the first animals to arrive on a new island. As well as carrying seeds on or inside their bodies, they carry insects and other tiny creatures. Insects are also blown to islands on the winds. As they increase in population, they provide food for more and more animals.

Land animals sometimes find their way to newly formed islands on rafts of vegetation torn from mainland coasts by savage storms. Others are brought to islands by humans. On remote islands, some animal species die out, while others are able to adapt to their new surroundings, and build up a breeding population. Over many years, new kinds of animals can evolve which are unique to their island environment.

Many kinds of island-living birds nest in large colonies on remote cliffs, to avoid predators that may steal their eggs. Puffins dig burrows to nest in, or sometimes take over deserted rabbit burrows. They dive into the water to catch tiny sand eels.

Giant tortoises *(left)* are found in the Galápagos Islands and also in the Seychelles, in the Indian Ocean. They have grown very large due to a lack of predators. Some giant tortoises graze on low grasses, and have a broad shell that fits close to the neck. Others have domed shells with high, arched openings, allowing them to stretch their necks up to taller vegetation. The introduction by humans of grazing animals reduces the tortoises' food supply and threatens their survival.

Large predators are often absent from islands, which means that some island animals do not need to be small and fast-moving. They can grow to larger sizes than their mainland relatives. It also means that some birds no longer need their escape mechanism of flight. Their wings become small and useless, and they spend all their time on the ground. This adaptation makes many flightless birds, such as the kakapo, a New Zealand parrot, easy prey when predators are later introduced by humans.

With a relatively small variety of animal life, competition between island species is reduced. One bird can eat a wide range of foods, which on the mainland would "belong" to several different birds. If more animals arrive, this lifestyle is threatened.

The kiwi is a flightless bird from the forests of New Zealand. It lives in burrows, coming out at night to feed on worms.

Insects can grow to huge sizes in island habitats. The giant weta, a kind of cricketlike insect from New Zealand, is about four times as large as an ordinary cricket. With no natural predators, it is flightless, but is now threatened by introduced predators such as rats.

53

LIVING WITH PEOPLE

ALL ANIMALS share the planet with human beings, many suffering the consequences *(see pages 56–57)*. Some, however, have learned to live in habitats that humans have created, such as towns and cities, or farmland. They have adapted their lifestyles to suit these new environments. Birds use roofs, gutters, and chimney pots as roosting and nesting sites, instead of cliffs and trees. Bats gather in warm attics or empty buildings instead of caves and holes.

The warm air given off from houses, offices, and factories draws flocks of birds into towns and cities on winter evenings. Many people enjoy seeing birds, and some put out food to help them through the coldest periods. However, birds and people also come into conflict. Flocks of birds are a hazard at airports, where they can be sucked into aircraft engines, causing damage.

The vast quantities of rubbish produced in a town or city also attracts less welcome animals. Rats, foxes, gulls, vultures, and even larger animals such as jackals, baboons, or

The feral pigeon *(right)*, so familiar in many major towns and cities, is descended from escaped domestic pigeons. These in turn evolved from the rock dove. Pigeons roost on rooftops, and have adapted their diet to include scraps and pieces of bread thrown to them by people.

polar bears, all scavenge from rubbish dumps in various parts of the world. Raccoons rummage through garbage cans in North America to get at the food inside.

Rats, along with mice, are found wherever people live. These adaptable animals have become pests, eating our food and spreading diseases. Flies, fleas, lice, and cockroaches also live close to humans, some also spreading disease, while mosquito bites are a constant danger in tropical countries.

KEY
1 *Raccoon*
2 *Gulls*
3 *Brown rat*

Other insect pests attack crops, or cause damage to homes and other buildings. Buprestid beetles *(below)* feed on house timbers, while clothes moths make holes in our clothing. However, some insects also have a beneficial effect on our lives. Bees are vital for the pollination of plants—in fact, much of the world's crop yield comes from plants pollinated by wild bees.

Other insects feed on pests which attack crops. Without the right balance of natural pest-controlling agents, however, pests can increase in number and destroy entire crop harvests. The use of chemical pesticides can upset this balance even further, as well as harming other animals.

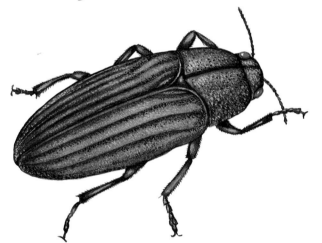

Humans have often created further problems by introducing species from one country into another. Rats arrived on islands in Oceania with the early European settlers, and became pests. To control them, the settlers brought in cats or mongooses, which quickly destroyed many of the native birds, small reptiles, and mammals. Rats themselves have killed whole populations of birds on small islands that had previously had no native predators.

Other introduced animals have competed with native species for food and habitat. The gray squirrel, introduced to Britain from the United States, has out-competed the native red squirrel, which is now found only in a few areas. Red deer imported into New Zealand compete with other grazing animals and destroy woodland.

Farming has made a huge impact on the environment, replacing woodland, wetland, and grasslands with cropfields and grazing land. Some animals have adapted to take advantage of these new habitats. Rabbits, mice, and many kinds of birds feed and nest among the crops and in the hedgerows of agricultural land.

ANIMALS IN DANGER

ANIMALS have always experienced rises and falls in their numbers, and many species have become extinct through a long, natural process. Since humans came onto the scene, however, the rate of extinction among species of plants and animals has risen dramatically. Humans have hunted animals to extinction for food or sport, and have driven them from their natural habitats. Some of the best-known animals in the world today, such as the tiger or the rhinoceros, are in danger of extinction. Many lesser-known (but no less important) species are also under threat.

Once common in many places, barn owls are rare in much of Europe due to loss of habitat—barns and other old buildings to nest in and hedgerows in which to hunt small mammals. Projects are underway to encourage the owls to return.

The illegal trade in elephant tusks is a constant battle between poachers and the wardens who protect the elephants.

People have always hunted animals for food, but unlike other predators, humans may pursue a single species ceaselessly until it has become extinct. Many kinds of whale almost became extinct during the 18th and 19th centuries, due to the high rate of hunting for their meat and oil. In a similar persecution, island animals, especially flightless birds that had no natural predators, proved easy targets for the first human settlers. With small populations and nowhere to retreat to, these animals were driven to extinction within a short time.

Animals are also hunted for sport. "Big game" animals such as lions, tigers, and elephants were shot as trophies by European hunters during the early 20th century. Today, songbirds in northern Europe are declining in number, due in part to hunting as they migrate across southern Europe.

The trade in animal skins to make fur coats or rugs has drastically reduced the numbers of cats such as ocelots and tigers. Rhinoceroses are killed just for their horns, which are used as medicines in the Far East. Only about 60 Javan rhinoceroses survive in the world today. Elephants are killed for their ivory tusks, which are made into ornaments. Young apes are taken for the pet trade, and the adults in their group killed. Despite restrictions and bans on these kinds of trades, illegal poaching still goes on.

Javan rhinoceros

In the face of these constant threats to wildlife, conservation programs are fighting to save as many species as possible. Wild plants are being gathered and cultivated, especially rain forest varieties that may have medicinal benefits we do not yet know of. Nature reserves have been set up all over the world, with wardens who guard the animals against poachers. Breeding programs are carried out among the most endangered animals, to try to increase their numbers. In the most successful of these, animals can be released into the wild.

Tree-felling in the Southeast Asian rain forest has deprived orangutans of much of their habitat.

Loss of habitat also puts many animals in danger. As more and more of the natural, wild areas of the earth are cleared to make way for housing, roads, industry, or crop and livestock farming, animals become isolated and have nowhere to move to if their habitat is threatened. There may not be enough food to support a population of animals, so they face extinction.

A relative of the lemurs, the aye-aye *(above)*, feeds on fruit and grubs in the Madagascan rain forest. It is very rare, due to habitat loss and persecution from humans, who think it brings bad luck.

Breeding programs in the United States have saved the black-footed ferret *(below)* from extinction.

ENDANGERED OCEANS

THE EARTH'S OCEANS contain a huge volume of water. Nevertheless, they have been subjected to extensive pollution in recent years, endangering the lives of plants and animals, and quite possibly storing up harmful consequences for the planet as a whole.

Many of the waste products that pollute the oceans come from the land. Modern chemicals that are sprayed onto crops to kill pests often do not decay naturally. Rainwater washes them into rivers, from where they eventually flow down into the ocean. Chemical fertilizers spread over fields also flow from rivers into estuaries and coastal waters. They encourage the unnatural growth of some kinds of algae, which reduce the amount of oxygen in the water and kill off other life. Raw, untreated sewage from our homes has the same effect when it is pumped out into the ocean, or taken out to sea and dumped. It also contaminates shoreline sand or mud.

The Kemp's ridley turtle breeds mainly on one beach in Mexico. Today, the numbers of turtles arriving to breed have fallen from tens of thousands to only a few hundred.

Chemical waste from factories, including poisonous metals such as lead or mercury, is allowed to run into rivers or directly into the ocean, or is dumped at sea. The harmful chemicals collect on the sea bed, and are taken in by bottom-living animals such as shellfish. The chemicals then pass into the bodies of the animals that feed on the shellfish. For the largest predators at the top of the food chain *(see page 4),* including humans, the effects can be deadly.

Gray whales used to live in the Atlantic Ocean, as well as the Pacific. They were wiped out, probably by whaling.

This illustration *(below)* shows some of the ways in which the oceans can be polluted. Chemicals sprayed onto fields (1) run off into rivers, and then into the sea. Some factories discharge chemicals straight into the sea (2), through large pipes. Others take it out to sea and dump it there, sometimes in large containers that fall onto the sea bed (3). A leaking oil tanker (4) can pollute whole stretches of coastline, while fishing boats (5) discard nets that are hazardous to many kinds of wildlife.

Other rubbish dumped at sea includes fishing nets and ropes from ships or boats, and household waste such as cans, bottles, and plastic. This rubbish, some of which takes years to rot away, can entangle and kill ocean animals, especially birds and mammals. It also causes a hazard to people and animals when it washes upon beaches.

Another major source of ocean pollution is oil. Tankers carrying hundreds of tons of oil sometimes run aground, spilling their contents into the water. The oil slick may be carried ashore by the waves, polluting the coastline. Animals in the water and on the shore become coated in the sticky oil, and many die. When the feathers of sea birds become clogged with oil, they lose their warm, waterproof qualities. The birds drown, die of cold, or are poisoned as they try to preen away the oil with their beaks.

Sea otters suffer from the effects of oil pollution in the water in the same way as sea birds. They rely on the air trapped in their thick fur to keep them warm and afloat. A coating of oil makes them cold, wet and heavy.

Other ocean animals have been hunted by humans. Whales were hunted for their meat and oil *(see page 56)*, while sea otters and some seals were killed for their thick fur. Sea turtles have become increasingly rare because they are killed for their meat, and their eggs are stolen to be eaten as a delicacy. Many of the beaches where they lay their eggs have been taken over by development or tourism. The turtles, along with slow-moving mammals such as manatees and whales, also suffer from collisions with boats. They can be injured or even killed by high-speed boat propellers.

Manatees *(right)* living along the Florida coast are often injured by the increasing numbers of speedboats found in this popular tourist resort.

Ocean life is also threatened directly by overfishing, hunting, and habitat destruction. Large-scale fishing operations, using enormous nets that can catch many fish at once, may cause some kinds of fish to decrease in number. This reduces the amount of food available for ocean animals that feed on these fish. At the same time, the nets may trap and kill animals such as dolphins and porpoises, turtles, and sharks.

The vaquita *(right)* is a small porpoise, found only in the Gulf of California. A victim of fishing nets, there may only be a few hundred left today.

GLOSSARY

Abyssal plain A large, flat region of the ocean floor lying mainly between 2.5 and 3 miles (4,000 and 5,000 m) below the ocean surface.

Adaptation The process whereby living things change their bodies or behavior, the better to suit their environment.

Algae Plants without true stems, roots, and leaves, found in water or moist ground. They include tiny, often single-celled plants known as phytoplankton.

Baleen Horny plates found in the mouths of some kinds of whale that filter plankton from sea water.

Bioluminescence The production of light by living things. It enables deep-sea fish to recognize a mate or to attract their prey.

Biome A large group of habitats that are generally similar to each other.

Biosphere The living world.

Boreal forest Dense coniferous forest covering northern parts of the world, including Russia and North America.

Browse To feed on plant parts from trees and bushes, rather than on grasses.

Camouflage The means by which living things escape the notice of predators (or prey, when they themselves are predators), by using their colors or patterns to blend into the surroundings.

Carrion The remains of dead animals.

Chemosynthesis The process by which the bodies of living things break down simple, nonliving substances to gain energy.

Climate The pattern of weather in a particular region of the world over a long period of time.

Colonization The movement and settling of living things into a new habitat.

Colony A group of one kind of animals living together. Some animals form permanent colonies, while others gather together only to breed.

Conservation The management and care of the biosphere, to avoid imbalances caused by habitat destruction and extinction.

Continental shelf The part of a continent that lies beneath ocean waters.

Continental slope The steep part of the continental shelf that plunges down to the abyssal plain.

Coral The skeletons of colonies of tiny animals called polyps.

Currents In oceans, the flowing bands of water that swirl around the globe.

Deep-ocean trench A long, very deep valley in the sea bed, plunging to depths of between 4 and 6 miles (6,000 and 10,000 m).

Ecology The study of how animals, plants, and other living things relate to each other and fit into their environment.

Ecosystem A defined area in which living and nonliving things interact.

Environment The living and nonliving surroundings of an organism.

Equator An invisible line around the earth, lying equally distant from both poles.

Estuary An area where a river meets the sea, mixing freshwater and salt water.

Evolution The process whereby species of living things gradually change to adapt to their environment.

Extinction The process whereby every member of a group, species, or subspecies dies out (becomes extinct).

Foliage The leaves of a plant.

Food chain The sequence in which a plant is eaten by an animal, which is then eaten by another animal, and so on.

Fungi Living things, such as mushrooms, that feed on rotting plant and animal material and reproduce by shedding spores.

Gills The breathing organs of water creatures such as fish, that extract oxygen from the water.

Graze To feed on grasses.

Habitat The type of surroundings in which a plant or animal lives.

Hibernation The process whereby some animals spend winter in a state of reduced body activity. Breathing and other body systems slow down, conserving energy.

Hydrothermal vent A crack in the sea bed found in certain places on mid-oceanic ridges, where very hot, mineral-rich water is released from the rocks below.

Invertebrates Animals without backbones. They include insects, spiders, shellfish, worms, and sponges.

Krill Small shrimplike plankton that form a large part of the diet of many ocean animals, including the great whales.

Larvae The immature forms of some animals, such as insects.

Magma Hot, molten rock formed beneath the earth's crust.

Microbes Organisms of microscopic size, such as bacteria.

Mid-oceanic ridge A long mountain range running along the ocean floor.

Migration The movement of a population of animals from one place to another at a certain time of the year, to feed or breed.

Minerals Nonliving substances made of natural chemical elements.

Nectar A sugary fluid produced by flowers.

Nutrients Substances (including minerals) needed to maintain an organism's bodily activity and new growth.

Organism Any living thing.

Parasite A living thing that depends on another (a host) for needs such as food and shelter, often causing damage to the host.

Pesticides Chemicals designed to kill or harm pests.

Pests Living things that cause humans injury or inconvenience because of their behavior or numbers. Some kinds of animals destroy crops or spread diseases.

Photosynthesis The process by which green plants use sunlight as an energy source to turn carbon dioxide and water into the sugars they need for food.

Plankton Tiny plants (phytoplankton) and animals (zooplankton) that float or swim in lakes or in the surface waters of the ocean.

Poaching Hunting animals illegally for food, sport, or to sell their body parts.

Pollination The transfer of microscopic grains called pollen from the male part of one flower to the female part of another (or the same) flower. This produces seeds that may grow into new flowering plants.

Pollution The disruption of an ecosystem, resulting from contamination by humans.

Predator An animal that preys on (hunts and kills) other animals for food.

Roost A place where flying animals such as birds or bats rest.

Scavenger An animal that feeds on the remains of food killed or collected by other animals. Scavengers are useful as they clear up dead plant or animal material.

Seamounts Mountains that rise 3,200 feet (1,000 m) or more from the sea floor, but which remain wholly submerged.

Temperate Having a mild climate, in between polar and tropical.

Tides The daily and seasonal changes in levels of the seas and oceans, due to the pull of gravity of the moon and sun.

Tributary A stream or river that feeds a larger one.

Tropical Situated in the tropics, close to the line of the equator.